The Usborne
Little Book
of
Dogs and
Puppies

First published in 2009 by Usborne Publishing Ltd.,
Usborne House, 83-85 Saffron Hill, London, ECIN 8RT, England
www.usborne.com

Printed in UAE. AE. Published in America in 2009.

The Usborne Little Book of Dogs and Puppies

Phillip Clarke

Designed by Kate Rimmer

Illustrated by Stephen Lambert

Digital manipulation by Keith Furnival

Consultant: Barry Eaton

Edited by Kirsteen Rogers

Internet links

The Usborne Quicklinks Website is packed with thousands of links to all the best websites on the internet. The websites include information, video clips, sounds, games and animations that support and enhance the information in Usborne internet-linked books.

To visit the recommended websites for the *Little Book of Dogs and Puppies*, go to the Usborne Quicklinks Website at **www.usborne-quicklinks.com** and enter the keywords: **little dogs**

Internet safety

When using the internet please follow the internet safety guidelines displayed on the Usborne Quicklinks Website. The websites recommended in Usborne Quicklinks are regularly reviewed. However, the content of a website may change at any time and Usborne Publishing is not responsible for the content of websites other than its own. We recommend that children are supervised while on the internet.

Contents

Man's best friend

Dogs were the first animals to become tame, or "domestic," and through the ages they have grown closer to humans than any other creature, earning the title "man's best friend."

Domestic dogs belong to a larger family of animals, including gray wolves from northern lands, golden jackals of the deserts, American coyotes, Australian dingoes, and foxes. Most wild relatives of dogs live and hunt together in family groups or packs.

Dogs belong to the same animal family as wolves.

The dog's tale

From tiny Chihuahuas to bulky St. Bernards, all domestic dogs are thought to descend from wolves. Starting as village scavengers, these animals were slowly accepted by people and, living alongside them, grew tamer and less wolf-like. They barked, their tails curved and wagged, and some developed floppy ears: wolves had become dogs.

Unlike a wolf cub, this Sheltie pup will still be barking and wagging its tail when it grows up.

Dog breeding

People gradually realized that dogs could make valuable helpers, and bred them to bring out their different skills at guarding, hunting, or herding animals. As they did so, distinct types of dog began to emerge: fierce, muscular guard dogs; slim, speedy hunting dogs; and, eventually, dainty lapdogs bred purely as companions.

Dog breeds differ hugely in shape and size, but they all share certain features:

For thousands of years, Pyrenean mountain dogs have been raised with sheep. As adults they live with their flock, protecting it from wolves. Their white coats blend in with the flock, and help the shepherds tell them apart from wolves.

Ears can prick up

Expressive tails

Cool, damp sensitive nose

Hairy coat

Strong, flexible body

Different types of teeth for biting and chewing

Paws have tough pads that sweat to cool the dog down.

Claws for gripping ground, cannot be pulled in

Once bred to protect carriages from highwaymen, Dalmatians are now admired for their looks.

Good breeding

In the 19th century, people started to breed dogs more for their looks than their skills. New puppies were registered with kennel clubs, who set standards for what each breed should look like. If a pup has a pedigree (a written family tree) showing that all its grandparents were registered members of their breed, then it is called a purebred or pedigree dog.

Pedigree pros and cons

One advantage of a pedigree is that knowing what a pup's parents were like tells you a lot about how it will grow up: its size, its looks – even its temperament. A downside is that it may inherit health issues common to its breed.

Like all its breed, this long-bodied, short-legged Dachshund may suffer from swollen joints.

Crossbreeds

If a dog's parents are different breeds, it is said to be crossbred. It may look like its mother or father, or a mixture of both. Sometimes, dogs are crossbred on purpose. Labradoodles are Labradors crossed with Standard Poodles. They were bred to be guide dogs for blind people allergic to dog hair.

Crossbred littermates may look very different from each other.

Like Labradors, Labradoodles have a gentle nature, and like Poodles, they don't shed hair.

Crossbreed names

Schnoodle
Schnauzer + poodle

Puggle
Pug + beagle

Cockerpoo
Cocker spaniel + poodle

Pompoochi
Pomeranian + poodle
+ Chihuahua

Borderjack
Border collie + Jack Russell

Peekapom
Pekingese + Pomeranian

This mutt has features from many breeds, including a Whippet's body and a terrier's tail.

Mutts

A mutt is a mixed breed dog whose parents are of an unknown breed, or are crossbreeds or mutts. They are often healthier than purebreds, and cheaper to buy – but it can be hard to predict how a pup will grow up.

Greyhounds' running skills have made them famous as racing dogs.

Dog breeds

There are over 300 breeds of dog, from pint-size Pekes to stately Great Danes. They are grouped today by their original purpose.

Hunting hounds

Hounds are dogs that were first bred for hunting, and some are still used in this way today. There are two main types:

Bloodhounds were first bred to sniff out animals for hunters.

Sight hounds, such as Afghan hounds and Greyhounds, are some of the oldest of all dog breeds. Their lean bodies and keen eyesight help them to spot animals from far away and chase them with ease.

Scent hounds, such as Bloodhounds, were bred for their sharp sense of smell. From the faintest trail, they could sniff out deer, boar and other animals for their masters to pursue.

Terriers

Small, fearless Jack Russell terriers were bred to chase foxes.

Terriers are mostly small dogs, first bred in the British Isles, to chase pests such as rats and foxes, and dig them out their holes. So don't be too surprised if you see a terrier chasing cats, or digging up your garden.

Sporting dogs

Sporting, or gun, dogs were bred to retrieve pheasants and other game birds. There are many types, with specialized jobs. For example, flushing dogs, such as springer spaniels, drive birds out of bushes into the open.

Pointing dogs, such as Irish setters, are gun dogs that sniff out game birds, then point toward them with their nose.

Retrievers, such as this Golden Retriever pup, were bred to fetch birds their master had shot.

Water dogs

This group contains dogs bred to work in the water. Some, such as Poodles, would pursue game into ponds and lakes. Others, such as Newfoundlands, worked at sea and were trained to pull fishing nets ashore. Today they sometimes work as lifeguards, helping to rescue drowning people.

Newfoundlands have a strong instinct to bring things ashore.

Dobermanns are strong, black and tan dogs first bred by Karl Dobermann, a German tax collector, to protect him from bandits.

Working dogs

Many dogs work, but the powerful breeds in this group were originally developed for jobs ranging from guarding homes, and driving cattle to pulling carts or sleds. A lot are heavy, large-headed types called molossers.

This puppy is a Husky. For thousands of years, teams of Huskies have pulled sleds for native people in the snowy lands of the north.

Border Collies were bred to work as sheepdogs, and many still do.

Herders and flockguards

Nimble, quick-witted and able to control animals with just a stare or a nip of the heels, the herding dogs were bred to round up livestock including sheep, cattle, or even ostriches. Flockguards are brave dogs that protect their charges from predators such as wolves.

Toy dogs

Small dogs bred purely as pets are often called toy dogs or lapdogs. Some toy dogs, though, were originally working or hunting dogs. For example, Dachshunds were first bred to hunt badgers.

Non-sporting dogs

Also called the utility dogs, this group contains a mix of dogs bred for various purposes, but which don't easily fit into any of the other groups. Non-sporting breeds include Chow-chows Dalmatians, and Bulldogs.

Pekingese were bred as companions to Chinese nobles, who carried them around inside their sleeves.

Bulldogs take their name from their original job of "baiting" bulls: a cruel sport, banned today.

Many non-sporting dogs were bred for jobs that no longer exist. Bold, long-coated Lhasa Apsos were first bred by monks in ancient Tibet as temple watchdogs.

Chow-chows are furry and bear-like, with curly tails and blue-black tongues.

Basenjis are very unusual in that they don't bark. Instead they have a yodelling howl.

Unusual breeds

After thousands of years of breeding, dogs come in more shapes and sizes than any other animal. Some aren't very dog-like at all.

Basenjis are a very ancient African breed, still used for hunting today. They are very clever and curious, fond of climbing, and clean themselves by licking, like cats.

Shar Peis are another ancient breed, from China, with hippo-like heads and wrinkled skin. They are strong-minded dogs, first bred for hunting and fighting. Their name means "sandpaper skin," because of their bristly fur.

This Shar Pei puppy looks like its skin is several times too big.

A Komondor's white hair falls into dreadlocks.

Mexican hairless dogs were first kept by the Aztecs, who called them Xoloitzcuintle (said "show-low-eat-squint-lee") and used them as living hot water bottles.

Komondors are big Hungarian sheepdogs whose heavy, white, corded coats make them look rather like giant mops. First used to protect flocks from wolves and bears, they are strong and courageous and make excellent guard dogs.

Bedlington terriers look more like lambs than dogs. These unusual dogs were bred in northeast England to hunt vermin, such as rats, and can run and turn very quickly. Not all Bedlingtons are white: many are sandy or bluish-gray.

The bushy tassels on Bedlington terriers' ears once protected their ancestors from rat-bites.

Chihuahuas are as small as kittens.

Dogs' bodies

Next time you go for a walk, take a good look at the dogs you see. It's amazing just how different they are.

Shapes and sizes

To look at the largest and smallest breeds of dog, it's hard to believe they're the same species. The tallest dogs, Irish wolfhounds, can be over six times as tall as Chihuahuas, the littlest.

An Irish Wolfhound can be as tall as a small pony.

Dogs' bodies vary enormously. Speedy hounds have streamlined bodies with deep chests, housing powerful lungs. Working dogs are thick-set and muscular. Dachshunds have long, low bodies that have earned them the nickname "wiener dogs."

Heads up

French Bulldogs have flat faces with virtually no muzzle.

Dogs' heads vary from extremely long wedge shapes, as in Rough Collies, whose foreheads flow smoothly into their muzzles, to flat-faced dogs with barely a muzzle at all. The shape of most dogs' heads is somewhere in between, with a definite angle, called the "stop," between their muzzle and forehead.

Ears and eyes

Dogs' wild relatives
have pointed, upright
ears, but theirs come
in many shapes, from
long and droopy to the
perky "butterfly" ears
of French papillons.

Dogs' eyes vary, too. For
example, Bull terriers have
dark, triangular eyes,
those of Weimaraners
are round and amber,
while Huskies' almond-
shaped eyes are often blue.

This Cocker Spaniel
pup has hanging
"drop" ears.

Many Old English
Sheepdogs have one blue
and one brown eye, but
these are usually hidden
behind their thick,
fluffy hair.

Like all Pugs, these
pups have expressive,
bulging eyes.

Legs and paws

Legs and paws can tell you a lot about a dog. Fast-running hounds, for example, Salukis, have long legs and narrow, hare-like paws. Northern breeds such as Alaskan Malamutes have broad, hairy paws for moving over hard, snowy ground.

Some dogs that were bred to work in water, such as Newfoundlands and Otterhounds, have webbed paws that help them to swim.

Although they are heavy dogs, Basset hounds have short legs, as you can see here.

Samoyeds, from Russia, have bushy tails that curl over their backs.

Tails

Dogs' tails range from the wolf-like brushes of northern breeds to a poodle's fluffy pom-pom. In some places, a few breeds of working dog have their tails "docked" (cut short) when they are young, to stop them from being injured at work. Docking just for fashion reasons is now illegal in many countries.

Coats

A dog's coat of hair may be long or short, furry or wiry. Breeds from colder countries often have two coats: a soft, dense undercoat, and a coarse topcoat. A few types, such as Chinese Crested dogs, have no coat at all.

From red Irish setters to black Labradors, dogs come with a vast array of colors and markings, some of which have special names. Brindle is an often-striped mixture of black with gray, brown or gold. Sable coats are pale with black tips.

Born white, these Dalmatian pups are starting to show their spots.

Poodle hair keeps growing, so it's trimmed regularly. This is a "lion clip."

Airedale terriers have a dark "saddle" on their back.

Bluish-gray coats with black patches are known as merle. Breeds that commonly have merle coats, such as Australian Cattle dogs, often have differently colored eyes.

A group of puppies born together is called a litter. Small dogs usually have a litter of around five; larger dogs may have up to ten.

A dog's life

From helpless whelps to playful pups, and from barking bow-wows to grizzled veterans, dogs grow up very quickly. You'll see great changes in your pet in a matter of months.

Early days

Puppies are born blind and deaf, and find their way around by smell. They stay close to their mother, who keeps them warm and clean. Newborn pups can crawl, but if they wander too far, their mother will soon bring them back again.

This Border Collie pup is just three days old. When it's not drinking its mother's milk, it spends most of its time sleeping.

By six weeks, pups have grown out of drinking milk, and are tussling with their littermates.

After two or three weeks, puppies start to see and hear. By three weeks, they also start to walk. At six to eight weeks, they've grown their first teeth and their mother "weans" them, refusing to feed the pups with her milk, so that they move on to solid food.

At four months old, this Labrador Retriever is "teething." Chewing helps him to relieve the ache as his adult teeth come through.

Growing up

Dogs don't live as long as people, and mature more rapidly. On a medium-sized dog's first birthday, it is equivalent to a teenager. By two, it's like a 22 year old. Each year after that is equal to about five dog years.

At six months to a year, female dogs, called bitches, are ready to have their own pups. At a similar time, males (just called dogs) start noticing females and become restless, even running away to find them. If you don't want your pet to have puppies, or to father them, you can take it to the vet for a simple operation. This is important, as thousands of unwanted pups end up in dog shelters every year.

Chihuahuas often live to be 15, equivalent to 76 human years. Irish Wolfhounds may only live for six years, just 49 in human terms.

Golden years

As they get old, dogs tend to slow down, and sleep more. Hair on their muzzles and bodies may turn gray, and some may develop health problems. Older dogs need less exercise than youngsters, but still enjoy regular walks.

Older dogs are less active, so they don't need such large meals as those in their prime.

Long-haired dogs, like this Lhasa Apso are only for those who have the time to groom them.

A new pup

For their first dog, most people find raising a puppy easier than adopting an adult. It is safest to find a purebred with a known background, but many people choose to rehome a rescue pup, even knowing the extra care it may need. Owning any dog, though, is a big commitment that will last its whole life. For a purebred, look at many breeds, and pups, before deciding. The national Kennel Club can recommend breeders.

Which breed?

It is vital to choose a dog that matches your family's home and lifestyle. It's also wise to investigate the adult version of the pup you're considering. A big breed may not suit a small house, and may eat a lot, which can be costly. Small dogs may take up less space, but some snap at little children. Dogs bred for work need lots of exercise and attention to stop them from getting bored.

Now it just looks cute, but this Border Collie pup will need a lot of exercise when it's older.

Meeting Mother

It is best to visit the puppy while it's still with its mother. A healthy, friendly mother is likely to produce fit, good-natured puppies. If the pups are mongrels, find out as much as you can about both parents.

A puppy shouldn't leave its mother and littermates until it's seven or eight weeks old.

A gentle mother dog, like this, who is happy for you to play with her pups, will probably have passed her calm nature on to them.

Male or female?

When picking a puppy, the differences between breeds are greater than those between sexes. Many people find, though, that females make calmer house pets, while males are often better guard dogs. If you already have a dog, one of the opposite sex is less likely to fight with it.

When handling a pup, use one hand to support its front legs, and the other its back legs.

Settling in

When you bring your new dog home for the first time, it may be nervous and excited. It will take time and extra care for it to settle happily into its new home.

A strong, plastic dog carrier like this is a good way to transport a pup to its new home. The small space can help it to feel less anxious.

Preparing for a pup

Before you bring a new pup home, you will need to "puppy-proof" your house, and decide where your pet's living quarters are going to be. Its food and bathroom areas are probably the first places it will need to visit.

Choose an easily cleaned place for your pup's water and food bowls, such as a kitchen floor. It will probably be hungry when it arrives.

Clear the floors of small items that a curious pup might swallow, such as hairbands, rubber bands or paperclips. Electrical wires can be dangerous, as a puppy may be tempted to chew them. Some house plants are poisonous to dogs, so make sure they, and anything else that shouldn't be chewed, are out of reach.

A quiet welcome

When your new dog first enters your home, it will
probably feel overwhelmed, so make sure there are
no loud noises. You can calm it down by petting
it, and starting to use the name you've chosen
for it. Once it has been to the bathroom and
eaten, let it explore the rooms, one at a
time, keeping an eye on it all the while.

Crouch down and
pet your puppy gently
along its head and back.

Meeting the family

It's good to introduce a pup to
lots of different people while
it's still young, but a room
full of strangers can be
scary, so let it meet the
family a few at a time.
Don't let children play
too roughly or noisily
around a pup, and
introduce other
pets carefully.

This pair shows
how friendly dogs
and cats can be.
At a first meeting,
ensure the cat
can escape to
higher ground
if it wants.

A pup's house training will be quicker if you're willing to take it to its bathroom spot at night.

Some owners keep their dogs in cages for part of the day, providing a safe, cozy den to eat and sleep in. Cages can also help house training, as pups tend not to pee or poop in their beds.

After some rough and tumble with a tug toy, these tired Brittany pups are ready for a nap.

House training

Whether you're training a pup to go to the bathroom in the garden or on a "puppy pad" in the kitchen, it will make mistakes. Don't punish it: be patient. Take it to its bathroom area after meals, long naps or playtimes, and praise it whenever it does the right thing.

Let sleeping pups lie

Like babies, puppies spend a lot of time sleeping, as their bodies use a lot of their energy to help them grow. You may find that they nod off at any time, even in the middle of playing a game. Let them sleep whenever they need to. They'll be making mischief again in no time.

26

Bedtime

Your pup will need its own bed. A cardboard box may be better than an expensive dog bed, as the puppy will probably chew it. Put it somewhere away from drafts and damp. If necessary, you can raise it above the ground with piles of magazines.

Washable blanket on top of newspaper

This box has just enough room for two puppies to curl up in comfort.

Making a puppy box

- 🐾 Find a quiet and sheltered place where your puppy will feel comfortable.
- 🐾 Cover the floor with newspaper to absorb any little accidents.
- 🐾 Line the inside of the box with more newspaper.
- 🐾 Put a blanket on top of the newspaper in the box. It will need frequent washing, so you'll need a spare.

Put newspaper around the box to help soak up puppy puddles.

Missing Mother

For their first few nights in a new home, a pup may cry because it misses its family. You can help by giving it a warm hot-water bottle. The noise of a ticking clock can also make it feel less lonely. Don't go to a pup every time it cries, or it will learn to cry whenever it's left alone.

A hot-water bottle wrapped in a blanket will remind a puppy of its mother's warmth.

Dogs' dinners

Puppies only have little tummies, so it's best to feed them several small meals a day. Adult dogs eat fewer, larger meals. Older, less active dogs need less food. If you get a new dog, to avoid stomach upsets, start by giving it the food it's used to, slowly mixing in a new diet.

A healthy balance

Good quality puppy or adult dog food will give your pet a healthy, balanced diet suited to its age. Low-fat snacks and meaty treats are okay, especially for training, but in moderation. Your dog should receive all the nutrition it needs from dog food, so it doesn't need to eat leftover scraps. Also avoid cooked bones, which can splinter and choke your dog.

Make sure your dog has its food bowl and a supply of fresh water in its own quiet spot. Try to feed it at the same times each day. Let a pup get used to eating with you around.

A Labrador pup like this one needs four small meals a day.

Puppy food has extra ingredients to help young dogs grow.

Chews are good for this puppy's teeth, and better for its health than soft treats.

Hungry hounds

Dogs' wild relatives hunt prey, but they often scavenge dead animals, and scraps, too. Upon finding food, they wolf down as much as they can. Pet dogs do the same, so their diet must be controlled or they grow fat and unhealthy.

Unlike cats, which need meat to survive, dogs can digest a broad range of foods. The menu on the right lists a few of the many types of dog food. There are many treats available, too. Ask your vet for advice on healthy treats for your dog, and never give it chocolate.

Menu

- "Complete" dog food provides a balanced diet for your pet.

- Kibble (dry food) is easy to store, and helps keep dogs' teeth clean.

- Some finicky dogs may prefer moist dog foods.

- There are also 'specialty' dog foods, such as those for sensitive stomachs, joint health, or weight control. Your vet can advise you on these.

- "Working dog" food gives extra energy to active dogs. It is unsuitable for house pets.

Your dog will need a health check-up every year.

Staying healthy

Like babies, puppies need vaccinations to protect them from diseases. A pup needs its first shots around the age of six weeks. When your puppy is young, it's best to introduce it only to animals that have been vaccinated.

Regular check-ups

To keep your dog healthy, you'll need to take it to the vet's at least once a year. The vet will give your dog a health check and "booster" shots keep its vaccinations up-to-date.

Unwanted guests

Fleas, roundworms and tapeworms are parasites: creatures that live on or in other animals, causing them harm. Puppies and dogs need regular treatments to keep these invaders at bay.

If your dog scratches itself a lot, like this, it may have fleas, but you can buy drops to kill them.

30

A healthy hound

Dog owners soon learn to tell when their pet is in good shape, and to spot the signs of poor health. Here are the main signs of a healthy dog:

Clear, bright eyes with clean corners

Cool, damp nose

Clean, pink skin inside ears

Teeth clean with no yellow-brown build-up (tartar)

Clean, glossy coat

Flat stomach

Paws free of cuts or blisters

Clues that your dog may be unwell

- Loss of appetite
- Lack of energy
- Scruffy, dull coat
- Black specks in fur may be flea droppings
- Gunky eyes
- Walking stiffly
- Having diarrhea for several days
- Dogs have "third eyelids" to protect their eyes. In most breeds, you only see these when they are feeling run-down.

Self help

Wild animals often know how to stay healthy, and dogs have a few tricks up their sleeves, too. If they are cut, they lick their wounds. Their saliva contains chemicals that kill germs and speed up healing.

Dogs lick their wounds to help themselves heal.

31

Short-haired dogs, such as this Dalmatian, don't need a great deal of brushing.

Grooming

Dogs lick and nibble their own fur to keep it spick and span, and sometimes also each other's, to strengthen their friendship. This is called grooming. You will probably use a brush or comb to groom your dog, but, just the same, it will both keep its coat in good condition and help it grow to trust you.

Coat care

Most dogs need regular grooming, but just how much depends on the breed. Short-haired dogs may only need brushing weekly, but long-haired types may require daily combing and brushing. Puppies don't take much grooming, but it's best to start young, so they get used to it.

Grooming tools

- Metal dog combs: finer teeth for finer coats
- Dog scissors: regular for grooming, or with teeth for thinning thick coats
- A carder, or slicker brush, is used to remove old fur.
- A bristle brush is for both long and short fur.
- Grooming gloves are especially good for dogs with fine coats.

Always brush a dog's coat in the direction it grows.

Hair, there and everywhere

Many dogs shed their hair twice a year: once in spring, to stay cool in summer, and then again in the fall, before they grow their long, winter coat. Central heating, though, often causes dogs to shed all year round, and poor diet can make their hair fall out in clumps.

Pomeranians shed their fluffy undercoats once or twice a year.

Doggy hairdos

The hair of some breeds, such as Yorkshire Terriers, doesn't shed, but grows all the time and so needs regular trimming. This can be very time-consuming. Some owners take their pets to professional dog groomers.

Like many of its breed, this Shih Tzu has been given a top-knot to keep its hair out of its eyes.

Claw clipping

Just as you clip your fingernails, most pet dogs need to have their claws trimmed. Dog claw clippers have a safety guard to stop you from cutting down to the "quick" (soft part) inside the claw.

This dog has learned to
"beg." Ignore your pet if it
begs when you're eating, or
it will become a pest.

Good dog!

Dogs don't know about human rules so
they need to be taught what is expected of
them. It's good to start training your dog
as a puppy, but remember that, just like
children, young puppies need patience and
understanding, and learn at differing rates.

Rewarding training

Training should be fun and rewarding for
both you and your dog. Whenever your
pet does something right,
immediately praise it, and
reward it with a tasty treat
or a game. When it does
something wrong, just ignore it.
Never hit your dog or shout at
it, or it will start to fear training.

Unlike you, dogs don't have a
sense of time. If you reward a
dog for something it did a minute
ago, it won't know what its treat is
for. Many trainers also use a small
device called a clicker to make a
sound exactly when their dog
does something right.

34

Teaching a pup to sit

First, hold a small treat above your pup's nose, moving it slowly back over its head. As it looks up at the treat, it will begin to sit down. When your pup sits, say "sit," praise it, to let it know you are pleased, and give it its treat.

Time for school

Puppy training classes are a good way to help you to train your new pet, and they will help it get used to meeting other dogs. It's important to choose the right class.

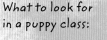

Teaching a pup to sit on command is one of its most important lessons. It could even stop it from running into danger.

Your puppy should already be used to meeting other people before you take it to puppy class.

What to look for in a puppy class:

- 🐾 A class that uses positive, reward-based training
- 🐾 An atmosphere where both puppies and owners seem happy and relaxed
- 🐾 A mixture of training and supervised play
- 🐾 Somewhere that isn't too noisy

What to avoid:

- 🐾 A class that uses punishment- or dominance-based training methods
- 🐾 A noisy, unruly class where pups are allowed to run riot

Walkies!

In order to be happy and healthy, even the most easy-going, home-loving pet needs regular exercise. Most dogs need as many as two walks a day, and a chance to run around without their leash, as well.

Every dog must wear a collar and an ID tag with its owner's name and contact details, in case it gets lost.

Like most dogs, this Golden Retriever knows when its walk is due. Dogs are happiest if exercised at the same times each day.

Getting ready

Once it has had its vaccinations, you can start taking your puppy out for walks. It will need a leash, collar and ID tag. The leash should be at least 1m (3ft) long, with space to fit two fingers between the dog's collar and its neck.

You'll also need to have taught it some basic obedience skills such as walking "to heel" next to you. Even a young puppy can be taught to walk to heel. Before you can let it off its leash in public, you'll also need to train it to come when you call.

Out and about

When walking a dog of six months or older, you might find it stops to cock a leg, peeing on trees or lamp posts. It does this to leave a scent message to other dogs that a place is in its "territory."

As soon as you can, you should gently introduce your pup to a range of different people, and other dogs (that have been vaccinated). The more new experiences it has when it's young, the calmer it will be as an adult.

Hold the leash loosely, but up out of your dog's way, as seen here.

Doggy dos and don'ts

Here are a few things to bear in mind when you take your dog out for a walk:

✓ Always take a "poop scoop," or an old shovel and a plastic bag, to clean up your dog's mess.

✗ Don't let your dog bark too much, pull you with the leash, or jump up at other dogs or people.

✗ Never let a dog off its leash in public places unless you are in a fenced in doggie park.

An extending leash lets dogs follow their noses when they're safely away from busy roads.

Making a splash

Dogs have a love-hate relationship with water. They often enjoy splashing in muddy puddles, but seem to disappear at bath time.

Doggy paddle

Like most animals, dogs know how to swim by instinct, although some breeds do it better than others. It's an enjoyable, all-round form of exercise, and a great way for dogs to cool down on a scorching summer's day.

Dos and don'ts

While dogs may be natural swimmers, you still need to take special care of them when they play in water. Here are a few tips:

✓ Always bring a supply of fresh water for your dog. You can't be sure that pond or pool water will be safe for it to drink.

✓ When you get home after a swim, rinse your dog with fresh water, and help it to dry off, especially its ears, which can pick up infections.

✗ Don't let your dog swim where it is deep at the waterside, as it may struggle to get out again.

✗ Avoid fast-flowing rivers, and never let your dog swim too far away.

Unusually for dogs, Basset Hounds and English Bulldogs can't swim. Their legs are too short to propel their heavy bodies.

Poodles were bred to work in water. Their name comes from the German for "splashing dog."

Puppies may be wary of water, and need to be introduced to it gently.

Bath time

Dogs clean their own fur by licking it, and will only need occasional bathing – although some mucky pups will need a more regular wash. Too much bathing will dry out natural oils that keep a dog's coat in good condition.

It takes two to bathe a dog.

This Schnauzer has shaken itself dry, but still needs rubbing with an old towel.

How to bathe a dog

1. While a helper holds the dog, fill the bathtub to about 7cm (3in) deep with warm water.

2. Avoiding its head, pour water over it with a plastic pitcher.

3. Still avoiding the head, rub dog shampoo into the fur. Massage it into the skin with your fingertips.

4. Rinse off the shampoo with lots of warm water. Then wipe the dog's head clean with an old cloth or sponge.

Roll on reodorant

Some dogs shock their owners, just after a bath, by deliberately rolling in the smelliest gunk they can find. Scent is central to how dogs communicate, so one that has had its distinctive whiff removed by shampoo may feel like a "nobody," and try to make amends.

Wallowing in filth is just your pet's way of reminding the world that it's a dog.

Doggy senses

Like people, dogs see, hear and smell, yet their experience of the world is very different.

Short-faced dogs can focus on TV images.

A dog's eye view

Dogs see fewer colors than people do, but spot motion better, and have superior night sight. Breeds vary, too. Long-muzzled sight hounds have excellent long-range vision, and a very broad field of view. What you glimpse out of the corner of an eye is crystal clear to them. But, unlike short-faced dogs, they can't see things right in front of them.

Like all dogs, this Irish Terrier can hear sounds too high-pitched for people to detect.

Hearing

Most dogs have larger ears than people, and much sharper hearing. Their ears act like funnels, concentrating sound, and can turn to focus in different directions.

The nose knows

First and foremost, a dog meets the world through its keen sense of smell. Dogs follow their noses to find food, but also to pick up scent messages left by other dogs. A pet dog on a walk often likes nothing better than to follow the trail of an interesting new aroma.

Just by sniffing, these dogs can tell one another's age, sex, health and feelings, and whether or not they pose a threat.

Dogs' cool, damp noses enhance their smelling power. Scent chemicals in the air have to waft their way up your nostrils before you sense them, and soon drift away. A dog's moist nose traps and absorbs passing odors, analyzing them at leisure with 25 times the scent-sensitive cells you have.

A dog's nose can pick up scents far too faint for a human to notice, such as a week-old fingerprint, or even electricity.

Canine conduct

Whether they're digging up the garden or chasing their tail, you may wonder why dogs do such funny things. A dog's behavior is a complex recipe made up of inborn skills that once helped its wild ancestors survive, the results of breeding, the effects of experience and training, and individual quirks.

Natural knowledge

Many animals are born with untaught habits called instincts, such as a spider's ability to spin a web. Centuries of breeding have altered dogs' instincts. For example, a wolf instinctively fixes its prey with a beady eye, stalks it, chases it, kills it with a bite, and eats it. A Border Collie will stare down, stalk and chase sheep, but has been bred not to kill them.

Learn with Mother

A mother dog patiently teaches her pups discipline, letting them know when they are out of line by ignoring them, growling, or picking them up by the scruff of the neck until they calm down. The best dog trainers are firm, fair and gentle – just like Mother.

Dogs turn in circles before lying down. Their wild ancestors did this to flatten the grass.

Pet dogs often bury bones and other prized objects, just as their ancestors stashed food to eat later.

By instinct, a pup will not soil its bed, but you will have to teach it where its bathroom is.

By play-fighting, these seven-week-old littermates are learning not to bite too hard.

If a puppy leaves its mother and littermates too soon, it will miss vital life-lessons, and may have problems getting along with other dogs.

Remember I'm a dog!

Dogs often become such a part of the family that it's tempting to see them as furry people who think like you. But dogs don't have ideas of right and wrong, don't hold grudges, and won't understand your words until you teach them.

Dogs feel no guilt, but this one has learned that looking meek calms down his angry owner.

Dog talk

Dogs communicate with sound, smell and body language. Learning a little dog talk can help you understand your pet a lot better.

Reading the bark code

Dogs bark for different reasons, and make many other sounds, too. Growling, whining, whimpering, yelping and howling all have their place in the doggy dictionary. Growling can be a warning that a dog's "personal space" has been invaded; whining may often signal frustration.

This Cocker Spaniel is barking for attention.

Talking scents

Before you've even walked into a room, your dog can tell you apart from other family members by your scent alone, and even know where you've been. The best way to say hello to your dog is to let it give you a thorough sniff.

Body language

Sound alone isn't always enough to tell how a dog is feeling. From an early age, pups learn doggy manners and body language to avoid risky clashes with teeth and claws.

A dog lying on its back is showing that it poses no threat (and probably wants its tummy rubbed).

Tipping its head to one side, this puppy is showing that it's curious.

Before two dogs meet for the first time, they show caution by approaching each other slowly, on stiff legs.

A confident, happy dog holds its head up, and wags its tail from side to side.

Upon meeting, they stare at each other, and may snarl and bare their teeth to say, "I'm unsure about you." The more confident dog will unwind first, look away, and relax its tail and legs. This calms down the more nervous dog.

When two dogs have overcome their initial fears, they make polite conversation by sniffing.

Playtime

Young dogs, like young children, spend a lot of time playing. They especially enjoy play-fighting. Not only are they having fun and getting exercise, pups are also learning crucial life-skills that will help them as adults. Playing with your pup will help it get along better with people, and get it used to obeying commands.

Puppies often bite each other in fun when playing. If a pup nips you too hard, say "Ow!" loudly, then stop playing with it for a few minutes. This will teach it to be more gentle.

This Bearded Collie pup is taking a "play-bow" to show it wants to have some fun.

A ball is better for your dog to fetch than a stick, as splinters can hurt its mouth.

Games to play with your dog

Some dogs, such as retrievers, will naturally fetch objects you throw. Hounds, however, may chase and catch things, but need to be trained to bring them back. Other breeds, such as Chihuahuas, may show no interest.

Many dogs enjoy playing "tug-o'-war" with a rope, or rubber toy. When playing, don't jerk the tug: stand your ground and let the dog pull. Remember to let it win sometimes, or it will get bored. It's important to teach your dog to drop the tug on command, and not to nip you.

A dog may growl when playing tug-o'-war, but its relaxed ears and curling tail show it's only in fun.

Dog toys

If you have to leave your dog alone for several hours, it's good to give it a toy to play with. A rubber dog toy will give it something to chew other than the furniture. It's best not to give dogs old slippers to chomp, or they may think it's okay to chew your new shoes, too.

From teething to ten months old, pups need to chew a lot. This rubber dog toy is tough enough to be up to the job.

Show dogs

Thousands of proud owners regularly parade their prized purebreds at dog shows, hoping to be judged best of breed, or even best in show.

Best of Breed

In shows, pedigree dogs are compared not to each other, but to an imaginary perfect example of their breed, whose features are listed in the breed standard. Show dogs aren't just expected to look good, they should also get along well with people and other dogs.

Dog shows aren't just for dogs with pedigrees. Today, there are shows for crossbreeds, too. At the Scruffts show in the UK there are rounds for Most Handsome Dog, Prettiest Female, Child's Best Friend and Golden Oldie.

This Pomeranian is showing some of the "points" that make up its breed standard.

Slightly oval eyes

Black nose

Tail turned over back

Long, straight topcoat

Small, cat-like paws

Pedigree titles

Pedigree show dogs have unique titles. These are different from their normal "call names," and many are long and fanciful. For example, the overall winner of the UK's 2007 Crufts dog show was a Tibetan terrier with the title Ch/Am Ch Araki Fabulous Willy. The first part means he is a UK and American Champion from the Araki Kennel. Of course, he answers to plain old "Willy."

Having been judged Best of Breed, this pedigree Afghan hound has won a trophy and ribbon.

Dogs on trial

Not all dog shows are beauty contests. There are competitions called "trials" testing agility and obedience. Herding dogs are often entered into sheepdog trials, where their owners can show off their working skills.

In agility trials, dogs have to navigate a complicated obstacle course as quickly and accurately as possible. Their handlers can run alongside them, but they can only guide them with words and hand signals.

These dogs are competing in an agility trial, showing how well they can follow commands.

Ding dong... Ding dong

Hearing dogs act as ears for deaf people.

Dogs at work

Dogs are much more than just pets. Many work alongside people every day as they help disabled people, sniff out missing persons, criminals, or illegal substances, and even save lives.

Eyes, ears and paws

Guide dogs are trained to help blind people get around safely as they navigate busy sidewalks and cross streets, even telling if their owner is about to injure themselves. Hearing dogs alert deaf people to phones, doorbells, timers and alarms.

Some people with physical disabilities have assistance dogs to help them in daily tasks such as opening doors, carrying groceries, emptying washing machines or even making the bed.

Many guide dogs are Labrador Retrievers (like this one), Golden Retrievers, or a cross of these two breeds, known for their gentleness and trainability.

Constable Canine

Police dogs are often called "canine officers" because their work makes them a vital part of the police department. An all-round police dog must be able to search for suspects, find clues, follow trails, and chase, disarm or pin down criminals.

When he's six months old, this Bloodhound pup can be trained to be a police dog that specializes in tracking people.

Working as police dogs, German Shepherds are very effective at deterring criminals.

Keen-nosed beagles often work as sniffer dogs in US airports.

Fire dogs

Fire investigation dogs are used when the fire department suspects arson – a fire that has been started on purpose. The dogs (often Labrador Retrievers) are trained to sniff out fuel, or other chemicals used to light fires.

In Russia, Huskies have been bred with jackals to create sniffer dogs with an exceptional sense of smell. These "Sulimov dogs" work at Moscow airport, sniffing out bombs, thieves and illegal drugs.

Seeking the lost

Search and rescue dogs are trained to seek out missing people, often in hazardous places such as mountains. They sniff the air, and follow any human scent they find, in what can be a huge area. Because they work by scent, search and rescue dogs operate just as well by day or night.

Ancient hunters

Native peoples in some parts of the world have been hunting with dogs for thousands of years. The Bedouin tribes of the Middle East still use Salukis, a lean, elegant, Greyhound-like breed, to help them catch hares and gazelle.

This is a Saluki, an ancient breed of sight hound. Many Salukis have feathery hair on their ears, legs and tails.

Furry friends

Therapy dogs work with people in hospitals and care homes. Just by being around, these animals' gentle, friendly natures help to cheer people up and calm them down, speeding their recovery. Many therapy dogs are pets whose owners have volunteered to make a weekly visit to bring a smile to someone's face.

Amazingly, dogs have been trained to use their fine sense of smell to tell if patients have serious diseases such as cancer. In the future, they may be a common sight in hospitals.

Golden Retrievers, like this, often work as therapy dogs.

Born entertainers

Dogs love to have fun and to please their owners, so it's no surprise that some have become professional performers. From circus dogs to stunt dogs and movie stars, dogs have been delighting and wowing audiences for hundreds of years.

Dogs are clever and eager to please, and can be taught all types of tricks.

Pampered pooches

Throughout history, some people have dressed their dogs to reflect their own style or status. You may wonder what the pets make of it all.

Costly collars

In 15th century France, Cherami, a Greyhound belonging to King Louis XI, wore a collar of gold and rubies. Lord Nelson, a famous British sailor, gave his faithful dog a silver collar that bore his name, Nileus, which celebrated Nelson's victory at the Battle of the Nile in 1798.

You don't have to spend like royalty to give your pet its own style.

This long-haired Chihuahua's trendy plaid coat shows that dog fashion is very much alive.

The lap of luxury

While many dog lovers treat their pets like honorary humans, some take things just a little bit further. You can now check your pet into a lavish, five-star dog hotel, buy it meat-flavored bottled water – or even its own cell phone.

This dog may look like it's sitting on an armchair, but it's actually a comfy doggy bed.

There are a vast range of accessories for today's owners to buy for their dogs, from bags and wigs to sunshades, giftwrap, pyjamas, and even wedding outfits!

Dogs on the catwalk

To some people, perhaps inspired by the example of celebrities, dogs are not merely pets – they are fashion statements. There are even dog fashion shows, and many top designers produce special canine collections for their style-conscious customers.

Heroic hounds

Dogs not only enjoy the company of people, but have also been known to use their tremendous protective instincts to save them from all sorts of life-threatening situations. Heroic dogs aren't just brave; they are also intelligent, calm, and incredibly focused amidst chaotic conditions.

A Golden Retriever named Toby saved his owner's life when she was choking on a piece of apple. He pushed her to the ground and jumped on her front, which dislodged the apple, then licked her face, which kept her from passing out.

Acts of courage

Around the world, many canine organizations and charities give awards to dogs that have performed amazing acts of bravery. There have been countless incidents of dogs saving people from drowning, pulling them from burning buildings, protecting them from muggers and other courageous feats. Some reports tell of owners being saved by their loyal pets but, on other occasions, brave animals risk their lives to rescue complete strangers.

Of all the animals that have received awards for heroism, the vast majority are dogs.

Mountain rescuers

Between the 17th and 19th
centuries, monks at St.
Bernard's hospice in the
Swiss Alps bred large
dogs to guide people
along snow-covered
paths and help in
mountain rescues.
The dogs, known
as St. Bernards,
used their keen
sense of smell to
find people buried
in the snow.

*St. Bernards, like this pup, used to keep lost
travelers warm by gently lying on them.*

Dogs of war

For centuries, dogs were trained to fight
alongside soldiers during times of war.
By the start of the First World War, dogs
weren't fighting any more, but were used
more indirectly. They carried messages,
weapons and medical supplies to and from
the front lines, guarded prisoners and
important military locations, found lost
soldiers, and sniffed out hidden explosives.

*From the Second
World War to
this very day,
dogs have been
parachuted
behind enemy
lines in search
and rescue
missions.*

Dogs in history

In 1957, Laika, a stray Russian mutt, became the first living being to be sent into space. The experiment proved that a person could probably survive being launched into orbit.

For many centuries, dogs have found fame, capturing the public imagination through amazing displays of devotion and incredible feats of courage. Some have gained legendary status and a few plucky pups have even changed the course of history.

Dogs that changed the world

Alexander the Great wouldn't have become so great if it wasn't for his dog, Peritas. During a battle with the Persians in 331BC, the brave pet jumped up and bit the lip of an elephant that was about to trample his master. Peritas was killed in the battle and Alexander went on to name a city in India after his courageous companion.

A Newfoundland dog kept Napoleon afloat, saving the life of the lucky emperor.

There might never have been a Battle of Waterloo if it were not for a fisherman's dog. A few weeks before the famous event in 1815, the French emperor Napoleon Bonaparte fell from his boat into the Mediterranean Sea. A daring dog on a nearby boat jumped in and rescued him.

Long journey home

After a Scottish Collie/English Shepherd mix, named Bobbie, became separated from his owners on a family vacation in 1924, he spent the next six months walking 4,500km (2,800 miles) across the plains, deserts and mountains of Western America to return to his owners. His home town in Oregon still holds a yearly pet parade to honor the determined dog.

After the death of his owner in 1858, Greyfriars Bobby, a Scottish Skye terrier, is said to have kept a constant vigil by the grave until his own death 14 years later. Since then, several books and movies have been made about his life.

A faithful friend

During the 1920s, Hachiko, a Japanese Akita dog, went to his local railroad station every day to meet his owner returning from work. Even for ten years after the owner's death, the loyal dog continued meeting his train each day. When a newspaper picked up on the story, Hachiko became a national symbol for family loyalty in Japan.

Akitas, like this one, are known for their intelligence and unshakeable loyalty, shown in the story of Hachiko.

Doggy facts

Here are some intriguing and extraordinary facts that you may not know about dogs.

Little and large

English Mastiffs are the world's heaviest dogs. In 1989, an English Mastiff named Zorba broke the records, weighing in at a massive 156kg (343lbs). It would take a professional weightlifter to pick him up off the ground.

By contrast, Chihuahuas are both the lightest and smallest dogs. In 2007, Dancer, an American Chihuahua from Charlton, was declared the world's smallest dog. He weighed just 593g (21oz) – that's about the same as a small bottle of ketchup.

Some breeds of dogs are easier to train than others. Here are the types of dogs that are the quickest to learn human commands:

- 🐾 Border Collie
- 🐾 Poodle
- 🐾 German Shepherd
- 🐾 Golden Retriever
- 🐾 Dobermann

English Mastiffs grow quickly – this eight-week-old puppy will quadruple in size over the next two months.

Little goes a long way

As well as being the smallest dogs, Chihuahuas also live the longest, surviving for up to 18 years. One of the world's oldest dogs, though, was an Australian Cattle dog named Bluey who lived for over 29 years, which is around 145 years in human terms.

In 2004, Tigger, an American Bloodhound from Illinois, broke the record for having the longest dog ears. His left ear measured 34.9cm (13.75in) long and his right one was 34.2cm (13.5in) in length.

Dog sprinters

Most dogs can run at around 30kph (19mph), but Greyhounds are the fastest dogs, reaching speeds up to 72kph (45mph) for short periods of time. Coming a close second are Salukis, which streak along at 69kph (43mph). Salukis are rumored to be able to run faster than Greyhounds but, as yet, there is no recorded evidence for this.

Salukis love to run, and take part in organized racing and chasing events.

Give a dog a name

The kind of names owners give their dogs varies from country to country, and age to age. It used to be fashionable to name your pet after a body feature, such as "Spot," or for its character – "Fido" was once a popular name, coming from the Latin for "faithful." Nowadays, many dogs are given human names.

Here are some of the most popular dog names:

UK	USA
🐾 Molly	🐾 Max
🐾 Max	🐾 Lucky
🐾 Charlie	🐾 Princess
🐾 Holly	🐾 Rocky
🐾 Poppy	🐾 Buddy

How to draw dogs

If you like dogs, you might enjoy drawing them. Their variety of shapes and sizes and range of body postures makes them the perfect subject for any budding artist. This colored pencil and marker technique is a fun and simple way to capture a dog's unique personality.

1. Using a brown pencil, draw a small curve for the head, and a long line for the neck and back.

2. Next, draw a short line for the muzzle. Then add a curved tail joining onto the back of the body.

3. Starting at the muzzle, scribble lots of little lines for the head and neck, and longer lines for the body.

Fine marker for nose and eyes

4. Scribble in the tail, legs and ears. Add a black nose and eye, then use a bright color for the collar.

By changing the line of the back and neck of the dogs, you can give them different characters.

Curved back for a sniffing dog

Press hard with your crayon to make a floppy ear.

Add a curved, pink line for a slobbery tongue hanging out.

Sitting dogs

If you want to draw a picture of a dog, you might have trouble finding one that will sit still long enough for you to sketch it! Instead, try using photographs as reference. Look for details of different breeds, such as the texture of the coat, or the shapes of ears and tails.

You can draw these dogs on cardboard or paper to make your own dog lover's greeting cards, notepaper, giftwrap, gift tags... the possibilities are endless.

1. Do steps 1 and 2 as before, but this time with a slanted line for the dog's back.

2. Scribble lots of little lines for the fur as shown. Add the front and back legs, and ears.

3. Add details of the face and collar, with tongue hanging out and motion lines for a wagging tail.

Press harder for different shades.

For a dog like this draw a long coat with no legs.

For barking dogs, draw another line under the muzzle, and some sound lines.

INDEX

Cover design by Joanne Kirkby

Americanization by Carrie Armstrong

PHOTO CREDITS

(t=top, m=middle, b=bottom, l=left, r=right)

2bl, 24tl, 27mr, 29t, 37m, 39mr © Jane Burton;

Cover, 1b, 6b, 7b, 8b, 9m, 12m, 13b, 14b, 17t, 18m, 22b, 23m, 25br, 28b, 33b, 34l, 36b, 41t, 43t, 44b, 46m, 48b, 52b, 53r, 57t, 60b © Jane Burton & Mark Taylor/Warren Photographic;

11m, 17b, 19b, 20m, 21tr, 26b, 31m, 32t, 40b, 43b, 45m, 47b, 54 © Jane Burton/naturepl.com;

15t © moodboard/Corbis; 50bl image courtesy of Guide Dogs; 51m © Valerie Shaff/Getty;

55tr © Petra Wegner/Alamy; 59b © amana images inc./Alamy